# Peanuts to Elephants

To EvanJohn
Thanks music
is a muse
Kint McAuliffe

To order additional copies, please contact us.
BookSurge, LLC
www.booksurge.com
1-866-308-6235
orders@booksurge.com

# Peanuts to Elephants

Kent McAuliffe

2006

# Peanuts to Elephants

# I'm the Dumb Toad

It's hard to fly, if they call you a toad.

1st day of school I had a test.
2nd I found out I was dumb.
They spoke not in words
But they said it all, putting me in LD.
They lied, said LD was not dumb.
To a kid words don't mean a lot.
LD did not mean Learning Disabled.
It meant plain Dumb to a kid.

Why teacher am I Dumb?
Is it something I said?
Is it something I did?
Or do I look dumb to you?
Tell me teacher please, TELL ME!

What do I do?
Do I fall because I am dumb,
Or do I work harder?
What, tell me teacher.

What makes me so dumb?
Is it my hair?
Could it be my faces?
Is my brain working?
Why can't I read like the rest?
The rest of the class can.
I want to cry bit I can't, why?

"CAT is spelled C-A-T class!"
But teacher, I don't see CAT
I see A-T-C, is this why I'm dumb?
I want to fly like an eagle.

The rest of the class soars,
Reading the <u>Cat in the Hat</u>.

You say I have what DYSLEXIA?
What does that word mean?
Does that mean I'm not dumb?
Is it good, or is it bad?
Tell me teacher, tell me!

# Dharam Bum

All set forth on desert floors
Looking for God's moan
Search for rollpoly sky
Set eyes outward to howl
For man's placement
In the chaos spell
Of the dream already...
Thought of by the one
In the game testing
Inward pulls for full skies
Painted in rainbows
Being the force
Setting us out of our
Standing high on tiptoes'
Nightwear drugged
Under flower
Pots growing older
Than the earth
For Buddha and Jesus
Brothers in the end
That come calling
In May's blossoms
The flowers show
To graves of lore.

# Entangled Yearning

Lucidity, white of the eyes
submerging the Idles
blue shores
circling the golden-
green translucent globes
Transfixed, the soul
From the old
past broken branches
Never let go,

Forming within
the river is let to flow
twisting out to
the ocean,
Drowning- water tainted
by the body's salt
branches once reaching, up
pull in
an acorn shell.
Love's true wind blows.

# The Beauty of Her Art

in your dreams or whatever art
you do is all reason *why*
is painted on the cave walls --
each stroke of your brush moves
inward to unlock the doors --
then explodes on to the stone
you have laid out -- on it is the
mushroom cloud of the answer
you so cavaliver'ly fought for

all poems -- paintings -- song--
books -- plays -- … -- …--
are samples of the being which
you created — the hydra walls
of your mind should be beheaded
by the storm of creative thought
because the artist who is high on
the white glow in moments of art
rages or dreams the sleeping body —
thechoas of her own alertness --

# Love in the 3rd degree

Opium den madness
Caught the foot
For there is no where
To run away from
Sickness of the heart
Palms savor of skin
Beyond the touch
Moment eclipse
Engage the disease
Of every breath
Taken in to feel
Escape of blood
Lost to the women
In her Sunday dress
For you to see
Discarded fear
Shoot outward
And inward to
The cave of forgotten
Lore of magic seen

# A lover's Howl

Why have you driven me there,
To the end of what could
have been that which I need.
WORLD wake up to me.
I give you everything.
Crazy, who me.
I think not.
It those cars that make everyone
so hard while I am to soft
Why can't I deal
With all the carve turns,
The ups and downs
are to lucid in me
looking in mirrors
I escape, To break
one open in let free
the true me.
To let go of all, thy.

To be free of insane demands,
No, one ever talks of the fifth sin,
Mediocrity, I know thy well.
It picks me for a friend.
Two years since I dance
with Mary Jane, now I am insane.
Holding on to the wrong girl
she does not love me.
Betrayed over
and over
and
over
once, again set free.
Did I ever ask to be free?

Should I come to the point.
I would but this is no litany
This is confusion spreading
like manure throw down
to make me grow.

Maybe someone will love me.
Maybe I could stop paying
        for some unknown sin.
God, I am sick again.

# Reaction

to our problems
we must come
out of free
to see the sun
and moon for
what the are
makers of myth
for what is
lore that does
not have a lighted
truth for all
to be within
there are no
stories missing
the piece of
unknowable
planes of a writer's
done deed of dish
water lesson for
time to test.

# Untitled

Two children
walking to the moon,
Interwoven to the 'Cross'
beckons to inside- Green Eyes
giving shiver
setting through bones rivers
four horse men glide riding
over curves to an end.

Bodies in water bend
under the white capping waves
Thought of self,
concave.

# Love Pains

A triangle breathe
Set in to the angle
Shot by bow
Arrow never found
For is it her wish
To be one with
Me the diseased
Of leopard figures
Cold is the touch
Like ice placed
In the crack of
A bone stopped
In place by the tingle
Of moments of bliss
Blazing forth for
 The first kiss
To stop the end
Of all other thoughts
To be as one in a cup
Transfixed in wed
In the truth of the all
Knowing purity.

# Recalling the Bluff

From cotton placed in the lips
sucking it all in, vision come within,

of the humming of a lamb set above,
the flight of two young doves,
to the place set up high,
from wondering eye,
she and I have forgotten,
the lucidity of the moment,
that still is, in form,
that there could be no end.

    the moon had a white glow,
    wind chilling the very soul,
    two children, yet to grow old,
    either that night were bold,
bodies enclosed from cold,

near a building grows a tree,
that made the past come to me,
in fever dream, caught
the glimpse of she,
now I know that she could,
never forget me,
and the moment of the past,
that is not to crack like glass,
forever she shall be within me,
always smiling and never to let go,

Form cotton placed in lips
sucked it all in, now I know.

# Untitled

the infinite rub
sets on in
to the cost
of never conning
again for it
was done
and there lays
like beached whale
eating pine cones

# Sight of Coyote

The moon out
At day is
A ghost lighting
Paths to night
As it folds
Over the clouds
Shadow of night
Shoot out at
The forsaken day
A coyote as big
As a large dog
Jumps its ghost
Like appearance
Over a farmer's
Fence in to
The forgotten wood
Could it have been
That I shall
The legend of
Trickery and magic
Coyoty the God

# For I Have Seen A Hundred Raves

Blue Mercury shoot
Down the overpass
Into a road where
Blackness fills the sky
In the day sun
Light could hardly
Pass through the
Bodies of the birds
That flew in all
Directions and caught
The golden sphere
In their breath
Almost a bird out
As the car wheel
Turn onto a straight
Road I thought
Has Matthew come
To take me home

## Pamoo the native inside

the first choas
warrior of old
naw how is
a bastard to
his great call
know in the
now of how
turkey bacon
is his fame
treat to eat
suckled by pig
feet in cold
of the Ymir
seasons placed
by the God

# Vision of Angel Gabriel

Holder of the fluid
Garden of right
Teacher of spell
The seventh gate protector
Given name by
Scribes in the desert
Showing the purity
Giving the sight
Of magic to us
The wicket mortal
Never shall I
Cast away this
Entity that bestowed
Vision of heaven
Away to me.

# Forest

always a sunny
beam of fathers love
for sweet kid in
trail of the park
gaiters circle
in the sea
of a calm smile
tricky for name
to delight the force

# The Saints Train Camp

To my nieces and nephus


    when,
Oh        the saints recalled you,

    when,
Oh        the saints recollect you,

    when,
Oh        the saints relocated you,

    when,
Oh        the saints remarked you,

    when,
Oh        the saints remolded you,


    when,
Oh        the saints revoked you,

    when,
Oh        the saints rebuked you,

    when,
Oh        the saints refused you,

    when,
Oh        the saints refunked you,

    when,
Oh        the saints rekindled you,

    when,

Oh         the saints rebooted you,


    when,

Oh         the saints rebuffed you,


I promise I well be in your number!

## of the little ones

There are daisies
in eyes of
beholden
mercy to
be made out
of childhood
for them we
hope and pray
for where is
stated care
balls and balloons
make a pack
to never be
broken on
backs of flowers
picked in may
for April brings
sweet paddle
to kick up
water shoots
up to cloud
coming back
down in morrow
robin eggs
sweet teaser
of myth that
is inborn to
them the little ones.

# Untitled

Children screaming in metal ward
for their mother and father
wondering which path
is nine fold the way home
never allied to see that
they have not meet me

# New clear melody for purchases

Going to highest
Beeper paged
For sale a item
On the stocks
Of markets
Treated to cut
For the wearer
Of this poem
For you bought
The book it is in
Hold in true kind

# Scholar and Gentleman
Poem in recalling Dr. Robert Joyce

A calm room
Turns it head to
The energy emerging
From the stage door
He has entered
Passion over flows
From a silent smile
As a voice from the belly
Begins to speak
On first day
He always said Fuck
The ancient youth
Father of us all
Mount to Dionysus
Laughing loads
Make your bones
Ache in meter
Man of myth
Mere melody
Of action born
Out of the boom
Of cave drawing
To the beat of
His own drum core.

# Untitled

At night the grass grows
And the moon glows
Saxophone enter my soul
Color turn to glue
Catching me
One call out 'bleed'
I grab at the moon
Lighting pure truth down
Fitting in my hand
Forced frown
Falling down, gone,
I crawl on this mud
Where could truth now go?
Clocks melt, 'tock'
Anyone know
Silent jazz stops
Nothing, but reaching out
To flowers
I am again low

# Nothing become All

A woman gave birth at the onset
of time.
Laid on the stabbed back
A child came,
to be.
smoke washed the walls
away
and the thundering crying
could be heard,
as hands placed Anew
into a crib.
reaching out,
to anything the child striking out,
slapped down with
a great
boom.

# Road Kill

Buddha does not talk.
Buddha does not walk.
Buddha hold his lily.
Buddha have no hands.
Buddha has no hunger.
Buddha does not gawk.
Buddha does not make.
Buddha walks on path.
Buddha have not feet.
Buddha have not land.
Buddha do never beat.
Buddha always laughs.
Buddha sings no song.
Buddha stand as tree.
Buddha is never seen.
Buddha is eight fold.
Buddha does not hate.
Buddha can not be me.

# Declaring a Wizard

The rain comes
As birds hum
Close to the ground
For what I know
Science does not
Tell for hidden
Knowledge of the rub
Spiders leave there
Outside weds
To safety before
Water beads them
Away from their sanity.

# Dragon in Mist

For inside it lingers
The great beast
A dragon on the dark
Side of my moon
Waiting to bite
At others to sleek
It's teeth into
Their necks and take
Away my sanity
Boiling in rage
It does not think
Of the means
To it's end but
Within all the pain
Lingers to be still
Once it returns to
Inside all is
Now safe.

# A bird's eye view

They chirp and sing
for is there never
white noise that
is not noise
but a gust rain
from the heavens
no trumpet
calling follows
home in the night
or is melancholy
all we know in
this experiment called
life the trouble soul
holds no truth gained
as a farm crops
disappear each year
another baby has
no choice as it
whales into being
yet the birds are
singing away our woes.

# Hawks and Starlings

a buzzard sit
in the road
dining on possum
that some hick
hit with his
truck as little
black birds fly
low predicting
that rain is to
come as a hawk
borrowed from
someone else
circles around
to join the bait
on the road
and God has
once again sent
ohms to me.

# Black Cat

Crossing paths
Keeping devils at bay
Searching for hope
Always sly
Never trapped
Pale yellow in eyes
Shine in the beams
Never growing old
Nine lives lived
Death's shadow
The rats end
Clear and slick
Trapping evil sprit
Away from it's
Masters house

## Mother  Cat

hot girl in
the wind of
my mind's eye
give the reason
to try in this
hour of own
delighted
feels that make
one known for
sanity
in this hold
mist of pure
engagement
set her sight
granted light

# Composer at his Keys

Chopping out notes
Each in the key
Of the places to hide
In a cave of care
To be a key
To be a note

What a delight set
Forth to the break
Ending in the might
Of mediocrity
To be a grand
To be a great

# Holding On

Grasping at
What is to
Be set forth
By the fate
Destiny stands
Silently in his
Garden waiting
For you to
Come into your
Own self-free
Image to be
See in the
Night's wear
Dreaded place
Taken off

# Life

Destiny hand
Guide across
The bow
A string
For the fates
To make seen
That no time
Has past since
The birth of
It all, bang,
And time sicken
Back to infinite
Words of wisdom
That never lay
Unfound as the go
Outwardly to
The four corners
Air the breather
Water the blood
Earth the craft
Fire the flame
For it is all
Done in March
For in spring
They come to
Lay flowers
On the grave.

# Art in display

Meagerly we crawl
from our homes
to the church
where poetry is
spoken for better
or worst we
listen to stories
of the saints
that are idols
to masses gaining
knowledge of how
to serve the glory
of the highest
bread is broken
in the cracks
of stained glass
and all the lambs
are in there
home of scared
truth of each
own desires
to be bettered

# Patches of truth

Sorrow surrounds,
Circles back,
Capture wrest,
Turn up X's,
Draw in sand,
That pumps.
In and thus,
To an end,
Of fates distance,
Seed shape into,
Bullets shot,
Around the door,
Knobs and bed's,
In the knowledge,
Doors close,
To reopen,
Magic is done,
Life is reemerged,
Sure way to hell,
As bathtubs fill,
No end to anything,
Just shot out,
In the night.

# Work In Pores of Paper

In the clouds
The answer lies
To all questions
For poet and knight
I be hidden in words
For outwardly I hide
The crust of the earth
In it I lay the way
Of others to search
Golden is the lamp
That set the seer
Vision outwardly
They capture the song
Forcing me to turn
Pens point down
To white spaces.

# The New World Writer

Trying to be Keats
Reaching out for
The nightingale
In mid night hour
Escaping the war
That is coming in
Morrow of middle
Times are not
Harden yet, in
The breeze some-
Thing stirs to be
Seen by the poet
All is not know
For future is
Unwritten to they.

# Voices of Lairs

Set from high above
The call out an end
To the thing that haunt
Never to deliver
The truth on down
The line of infinite
Tracks of blues
Seem to be placed
On in the side door
Of notes sung out
To be repeated over
And over again

# The Cost

To care is
Knowing
Of closed door
Mistakes done
In the debate
Of life between
Two kindred
Souls that grow
To each other
In the twilight
That is evening
That creates
New love
Outside old
Caring takes
Time to trust
The misery of
A Girl of Grails
Golden youth
Capture in cup
Wood holding
Meaning for us

# Mind

A small thought
One must hold
The right key
To open doorways

# Body

A small thought
One must tell
The way in
To open doorways

# Soul

A small thought
One must heed
The tiny truth
To open doorways

# My bate

trying to top myself
mundane set in
a smoke in the rub
coke to shock the block
what more to say
pissing in wind
to the thin
winter is coming
level two in gates
what is the stop
of this sick break

# My mind

Twist in turns
Inside it is a cave
Of unveil decries
That is ample
With lies
Tell me I am some-
Thing great
Pass my own
Mediocrity.

# Composer at his Keys

Chopping out notes
Each in the key
Of the places to hide
In a cave of care
To be a key
To be a note

What a delight set
Forth to the break
Ending in the might
Of mediocrity
To be a grand
To be a great

# New clear melody for purchases

Going to highest
Beeper paged
For sale a item
On the stocks
Of markets
Treated to cut
For the wearer
Of this poem
For you bought
The book it is in
Hold in true kind

# Whiskey and cola

setting up drinks
the band starts
and all ladies
are looking
backwards up
down it goes
liking the taste
make all other
flavors benign
trapping the teeth
numb to bone
cranking taste
of pure engaged
enjoyment sing
to Dandy boy
green glass
of brown water

# Sportsmen's bar

Deer hung for
All to transpire
Under the race
Of million coins
Throw to the cellar
Door left a jar
Pickled in eggs
Taste so sweet
From pigs feet
That never leaves
The window sill
Capturing dragons
In sweet melodies